pre-te pathways

A Journey Through Proverbs

Daily Steps to grow in wisdom!

by Casandra Pardine

MW01533555

Scripture taken from the New King James Version®. Copyright © 1982 by Thomas Nelson. Used by permission. All rights reserved.

Copyright © 2024 Casandra Pardine.
All rights reserved.

No portion of this book may be reproduced in any form without written permission from the publisher or author, except as permitted by U.S. copyright law.

ISBN 9798304639248

Dedication

To my husband, Eric, the love of my life. Thank you for inspiring me to always use my talents for Jesus and for being my greatest encourager. Your unwavering support and patient guidance as my "grammar king" have been invaluable. I am so grateful for all the years you've spent lovingly editing my work and cheering me on. This book is as much a testament to your love and faith as it is to mine.

A daughter of the King is a girl who wants to follow God and learn more from His Word. May this book help you on your walk with the King of Kings!

This book belongs to

_____

Daughter of the King!

TABLE OF CONTENTS

Proverbs

Day 1: Start with Wisdom

Day 2: Listen to Wisdom

Day 3: Guard Your Heart

Day 4: Treasure Wisdom

Day 5: Trust the Giver of Wisdom

Day 6: Seek God's Wisdom

Day 7: The Path of the Righteous

Day 8: God is Your Shield

Day 9: Humility and Honor

Day 10: Kind Words

Day 11: God's Wisdom Stands

Day 12: Work on Soft Answers

Day 13: Walk with the Wise

Day 14: Looking at the Heart

Day 15: Righteous Fruit

Day 16: Powerful Words

Day 17: More Than Skin Deep

Day 18: Prideful Attitudes

Day 19: A Friend Loves

Day 20: Walking with Integrity

Day 21: Hard Work Pays Off

Day 22: Wisdom Protects You

Day 23: Be Slow to Anger

Day 24: Honor Your Parents

Day 25: Avoid Gossip

Day 26: God Directs Your Path

Day 27: True Friendship

Day 28: The Best Policy

Day 29: Trust God's Protection

Day 30: Living for God

Notes

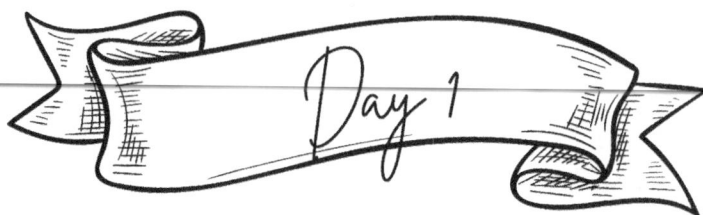

Start with Wisdom

"The Fear of the Lord is the beginning of knowledge, but fools despise wisdom and instruction." Proverbs 1:7 (NKJV)

Reflect on the passage...

A wise girl respects God and his Word. Wisdom comes from directly applying God's Word to my life. How do I know what is the right thing or the wrong thing to do? I must know God's Word to know gain God's wisdom. The foolish person pretends like they don't need God's instructions on how to live our lives! Do you want to be wise? Open up your Bible and learn how to live your life from the One who gave it to you!

Day 1

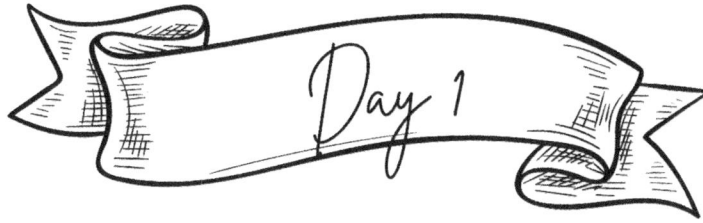

Share your thoughts!

_____

_____

_____

_____

_____

_____

Challenge yourself!

A great way to start your day is by asking God for wisdom! Begin each day this month by asking God for wisdom in your choices and decisions. Take a moment to pray before starting your day.

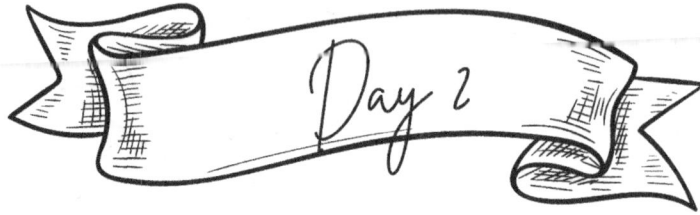

Listen to Wisdom

"But whoever listens to me will dwell safely, and will be secure, without fear of evil." Proverbs 1:33 (NKJV)

Reflect on the passage...

Safe and secure! That's God's promise to you when you listen to His wisdom and follow it. Do you want to live in peace and be free from fear and worry? Then choose God's way over your own way! Those who turn away from God's wisdom are doomed to fail. Choose the fear of the Lord and live safe inside His plan for you.

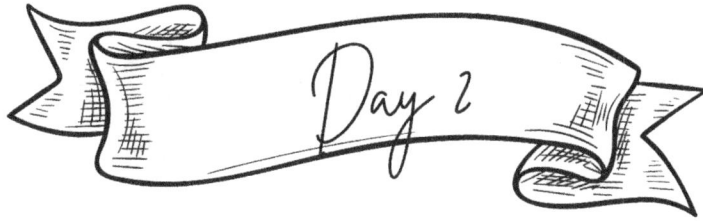

Share your thoughts!

_____

_____

_____

_____

_____

_____

_____

Challenge yourself!

Think about an area of your life where you need to listen to God more. Write it down and ask Him to help you consistently listen. Come back in a week and record how you did!

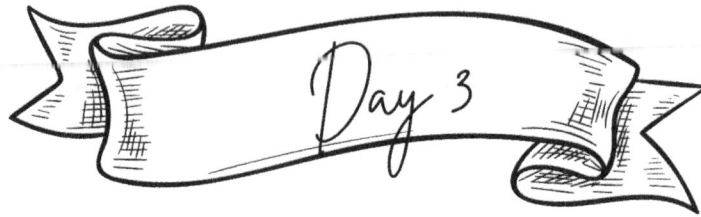

Guard Your Heart

"Keep your heart with all diligence, for out of it spring the issues of life." Proverbs 4:23 (NKJV)

Reflect on the passage...

The world says, "Trust you heart. Follow you heart. Do what your heart is telling you to do!" God says the heart is desperately wicked so you need to keep your heart and guard your heart. Keep it where? Centered on His Word. Guard it from whay? From anything and everything that would want to influence you to take your focus off of God. Be careful what you let in—what you watch, listen to, and think about.

Day 3

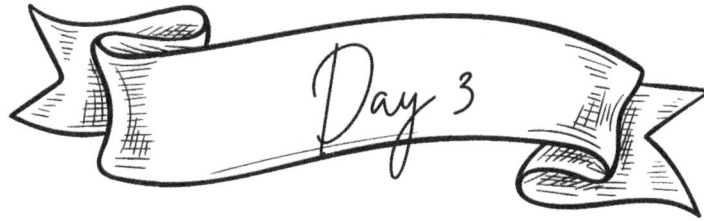

Share your thoughts!

_____
_____
_____
_____
_____
_____
_____

Challenge yourself!

Evaluate your daily habits, such as what you consume on social media. Who or what is controlling your heart? What steps can you take to protect your heart better? List a few above!

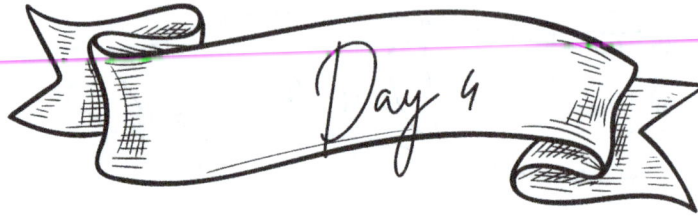

Treasure Wisdom

"If you seek her as silver, and search for her as for hidden treasures..." Proverbs 2:4 (NKJV)

Reflect on the passage...

What does that word "if" mean in our verse today? When you see an "if" in the Bible look for a "then". It is in verse 5, If you seek for wisdom you will find understand the fear of the Lord and find the knowledge of God! Verse 7 says that God has stored it up for you! But first you have to seek it. Read all of Proverbs chapter 2 to help you seek the most valuable treasure ever found! It is definitely worth the effort!

Day 4

Share your thoughts!

_____

_____

_____

_____

_____

_____

_____

Challenge yourself!

Make time for prayer and reading your Bible. Search for God's wisdom as though it were hidden treasure! Write down a part of God's wisdom today.

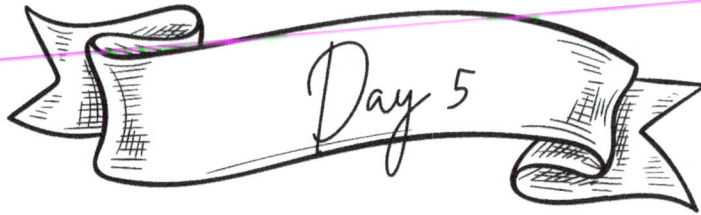

Trust the Giver of Wisdom

"Trust in the Lord with all your heart, and lean not on your own understanding; in all your ways acknowledge Him, and He shall direct your paths." Proverbs 3:5-6 (NKJV)

Reflect on the passage...

Well today's passage seems pretty easy to understand! When we trust God we are relying on Him completely, even when things don't make sense. Have you ever had to trust Him in a situation where you didn't know the outcome? Sometimes things don't go the way we plan, but when you put your faith in Him, you can trust that He will guide you and will be with you through it all.

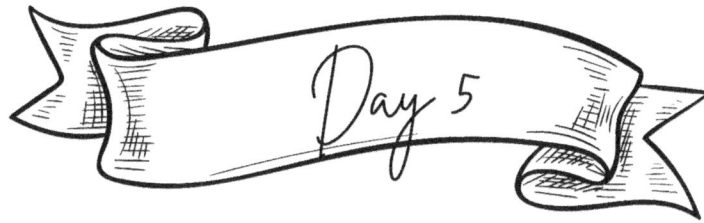

Share your thoughts!

_____

_____

_____

_____

_____

_____

Challenge yourself!

What is one area where you are finding it hard to trust God? School, relationships, diet, friends, parents, anxiety? Surrender it to Him in prayer today and ask for His guidance. Seek help from a trusted source and ask for prayer today!

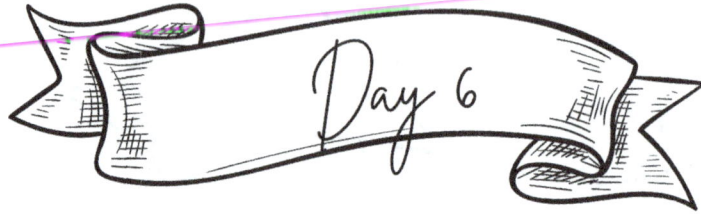

Seek God's Wisdom

"For the Lord gives wisdom; from His mouth come knowledge and understanding."

Proverbs 2:6 (NKJV)

Reflect on the passage...

Okay! Time for a pop quiz! Who gives you wisdom? If you asnwered, "God!" you get a 100%! We can't take credit for any of it. He is the source of knowledge and understanding. God is the giver of good gifts. If you need wisdom (and we all do) ask God! He has it in abundant supply. Ask Him to give you the wisdom to face your challenges today!

Day 6

Share your thoughts!

_____

_____

_____

_____

_____

_____

Challenge yourself!

Spend some time today reading Proverbs. If you read chapter 2 on Day 4, then read chapter 3. Reading a chapter of Proverbs a day is a great way to grow in wisdom! Ask God to speak to you through His Word.

The Path of the Righteous

"But the path of the just is like the shining sun, that shines ever brighter unto the perfect day."

Proverbs 4:18 (NKJV)

Reflect on the passage...

Have you ever been at a point in your life where bad decisions have just made your life seem dark like a stormy day full of bad weather? This passage reminds us that the lives of those who do what is right are like the brightness of the shining sun shining all the way to a perfect day! When you live like Jesus it feels like the warm sun shining down on you filling your heart with gladness. Choose to follow God's wisdom today and shine like the Son!

Share your thoughts!

_____

_____

_____

_____

_____

_____

_____

Challenge yourself!

How can you make your path brighter today by following God more closely? If you don't know how, ask God to show you how and He will! Commit to taking a small step of faith today.

God is Your Shield

"Every word of God is pure; He is a shield to those who put their trust in Him." Proverbs 30:5 (NKJV)

Reflect on the passage...

What does it mean to say that God's Word is pure? It means that it is 100% truth and we can trust it. We can also trust the One Who gave us His Word. Today's verse reminds us that trusting God provides protection for us. Why do you think that is? Could it be because He wants the best for our lives? What is one truth from the Bible you are trusting in today?

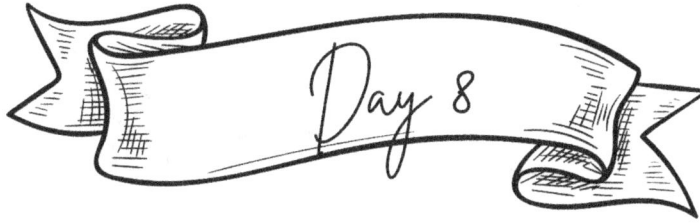

Share your thoughts!

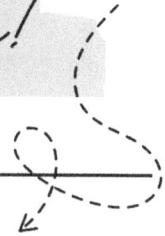

_____

_____

_____

_____

_____

_____

_____

Challenge yourself!

Do you have fears or anxieties today? When we don't know what the future holds it can be hard to trutst! Pray and ask God to be your shield, trusting in His promises. He is always trustworthy.

Humility and Honor

"The fear of the Lord is the instruction of wisdom, and before honor is humility." Proverbs 15:33 (NKJV)

Reflect on the passage...

Have you ever heard someone talk about how they needed to be respected by others? We need to understand that to fear the Lord does not mean to cower in the corner, but to honor, respect and reverence Him. If you desire for others to honor and respect you the key is to be humble. God values a humble heart that reveres Him.

Share your thoughts!

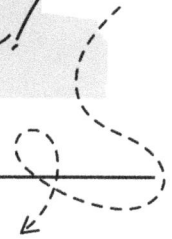

_____

_____

_____

_____

_____

_____

_____

Challenge yourself!

Ask yourself if there's any area where you need to practice humility, whether in friendships, school, or family relationships. Write it down above and make a plan to work on it.

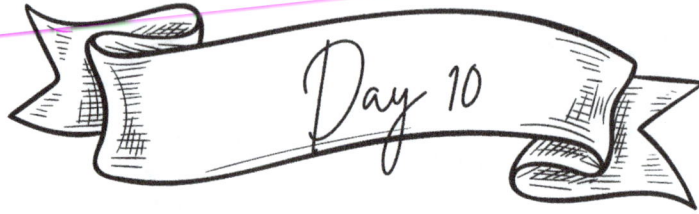

Kind Words

"Pleasant words are like a honeycomb, sweetness to the soul and health to the bones."

Proverbs 16:24 (NKJV)

Reflect on the passage...

The bees that you see busily working in the summer spend a lot of energy flying back and forth to build up the honeycomb and make the sweet, sweet honey we love and enjoy. Your words have power. When your words are kind they bring healing, encouragement, and life to others. Choose to use your words wisely. Be busy bringing pleasant sweetness to the souls of others!

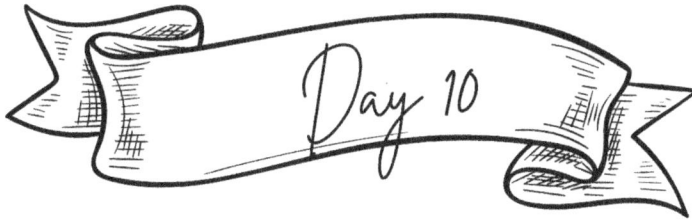

Share your thoughts!

_____

_____

_____

_____

_____

_____

Challenge yourself!

Go out of your way to bring sweetness into the lives of others today. Make a list of peple who you will intentionally bless with kind words and make it happen!

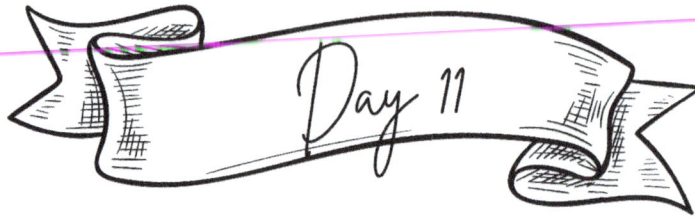

God's Wisdom Stands

"There are many plans in a man's heart, nevertheless the Lord's counsel-that will stand."

Proverbs 19:21 (NKJV)

Reflect on the passage...

Sometimes we have our life perfectly planned out, and then...Plop! Suddenly, everything gets turned upside down. The best plan to follow is God's plan and you should ask Him for wisdom in all of your decisions. God's purpose will always prevail. Trust His wisdom, even when your plans change.

Share your thoughts!

_____

_____

_____

_____

_____

_____

Challenge yourself!

Instead of trying to perfectly plan out your life, ask God to guide your steps today. What are you holding onto that you need to let go of. Pray, and give your plans over to God. He knows what's best for you!

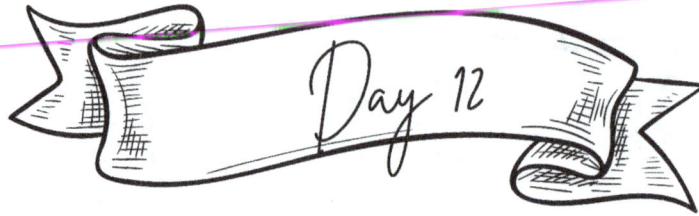

Work on Soft Answers

"A soft answer turns away wrath, but a harsh word stirs up anger." Proverbs 15:1 (NKJV)

Reflect on the passage...

Think about the way you respond to others. Can you hear those words playing back in your head? Did they help the situation? You can either calm a situation or make it worse not only by your word choice but also by the tone of your voice. Choosing a gentle response can bring peace. How will you choose to respond today?

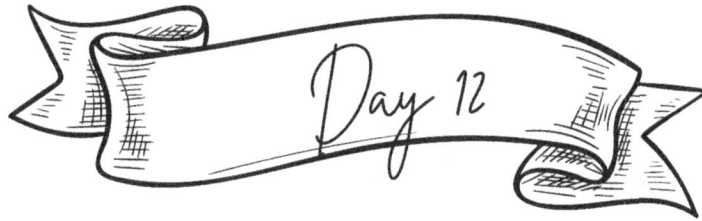

Share your thoughts!

_____

_____

_____

_____

_____

_____

_____

Challenge yourself!

You cannot control what others do or say, but you can control your response. Write down some good ways to respond to the things that usually upset you. Have a plan to give a soft answer that pleases the Lord!

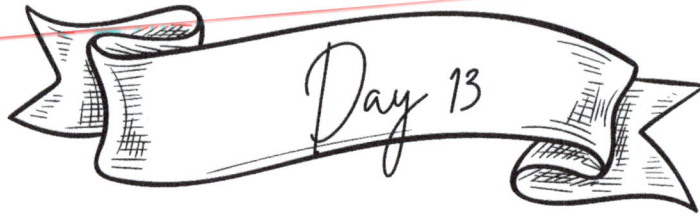

Walk with the Wise

"He who walks with wise men will be wise, but the companion of fools will be destroyed."

Proverbs 13:20 (NKJV)

Reflect on the passage...

Have you ever heard the saying, "You become like those you hang around"? Well, it turns out that the Bible has something to say about choosing your friends. If you choose wise friends they will encourage you to be wise. If you choose to hang out with those who do foolish things, guess what, you just might find yourself in a world of trouble!

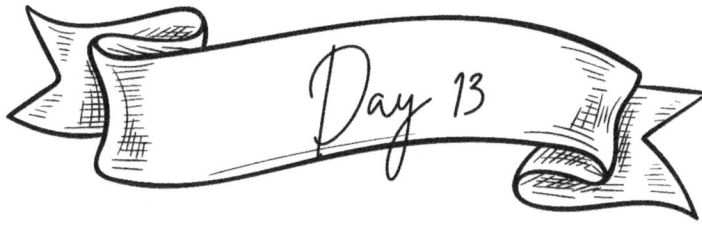

Share your thoughts!

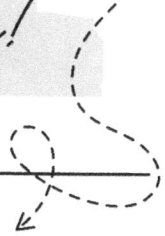

_____

_____

_____

_____

_____

_____

Challenge yourself!

Reflect on your friendships. Are they helping you grow closer to God? You should seek relationships that lead you toward wisdom instead of foolish actions. You can also be the change you want to see! Who can you influence wisely today?

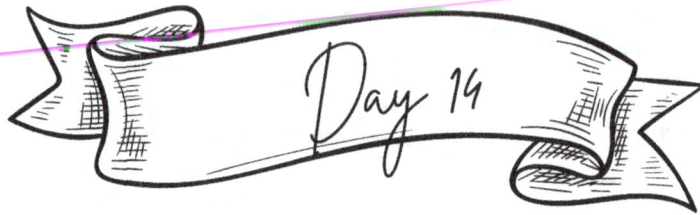

Looking at the Heart

"Every way of a man is right in his own eyes, but the Lord weighs the hearts." Proverbs 21:2 (NKJV)

Reflect on the passage...

It is very easy to justify your own actions. I mean, if I thought it up it can't be all that bad, right? Wrong! Our hearts can deceive us, so we need a better way to judge our actions than our feelings. God looks at our heart in the sense that He judges our true motivation. Are we living for Him or for ourselves?

Day 14

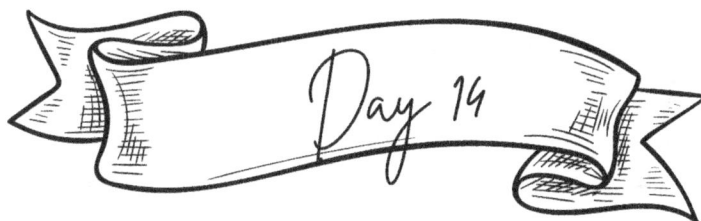

Share your thoughts!

_____

_____

_____

_____

_____

_____

_____

Challenge yourself!

Take some time to think about why you do the things you do. Is it because you want to bring glory to God or are your motives purely selfish? Ask God to help you evaluate how you are living your life. Is there anything you need to change?

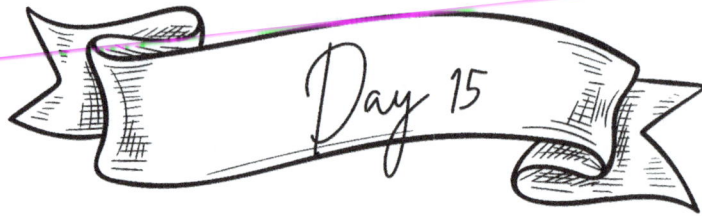

Righteous Fruit

"The fruit of the righteous is a tree of life, and he who wins souls is wise." Proverbs 11:30 (NKJV)

Reflect on the passage...

If you live your life for God you should be producing good fruit. What kind of fruit is that? Apples? Oranges? Bananas? Nope. Spiritual fruit that comes from knowing God and sharing what you know about Him with those around you. When you tell others how they can find eternal life in Jesus, you can impact their lives for all eternity.

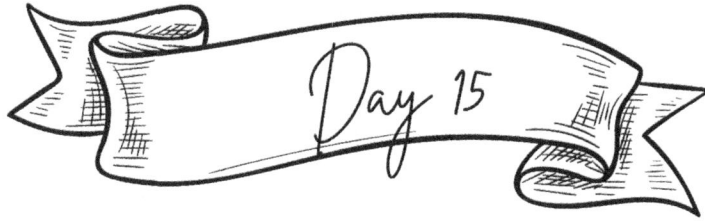

Share your thoughts!

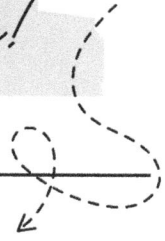

_____

_____

_____

_____

_____

_____

_____

Challenge yourself!

Think of some people you can encourage to know God more. Write down their names praying for opportunities to share what's on your heart. Reach out to one of them today. It can be as simple as sharing a verse or what God has done for you!

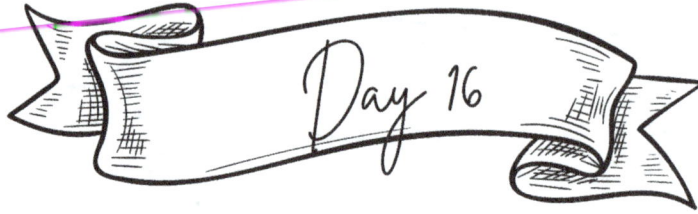

Powerful Words

"Death and life are in the power of the tongue, and those who love it will eat its fruit."

Proverbs 18:21 (NKJV)

Reflect on the passage...

The tongue is one of the most powerful weapons on earth! You can build someone up or tear them down in an instant. That's some power! However, once those words leave your mouth you can't shove them back in. No one should wield a powerful weapon without knowing how to use it. You must carefully choose how you use the power that you have been given.

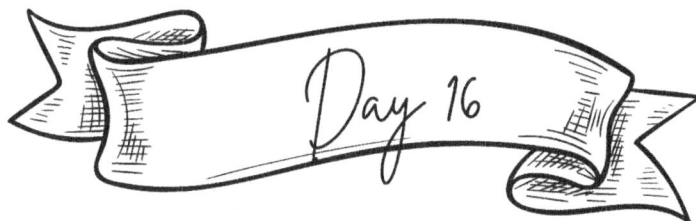

Share your thoughts!

_____

_____

_____

_____

_____

_____

Challenge yourself!

How will you use your superpower today? Challenge yourself to speak positive and encouraging words. Don't fall into the deady spiral of gossip, harsh words and negativity. Write down an encouraging phrase to use today.

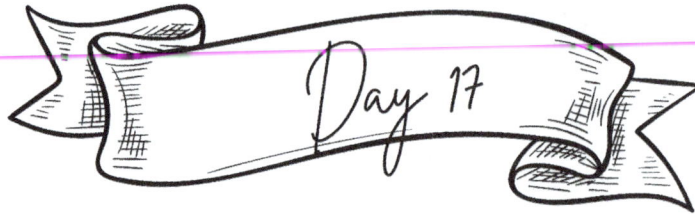

More Than Skin Deep

"Charm is deceitful and beauty is passing, but a woman who fears the Lord, she shall be praised."

Proverbs 31:30 (NKJV)

Reflect on the passage...

Take a moment to look in the mirror. Whatever you see there, whether you like it or not, doesn't matter. Why? Because pretty soon it will be different. Our outward beauty changes and fades as the days go by. God says that we should focus on inward beauty. If you allow God to work in your heart your inward beauty will be reflected on the outside!

Share your thoughts!

_____

_____

_____

_____

_____

_____

Challenge yourself!

What inner qualities do you want to develop to honor God? Trying to change everything at once is too much to handle! Choose one quality to start working on today. Ask God to help you live for Him!

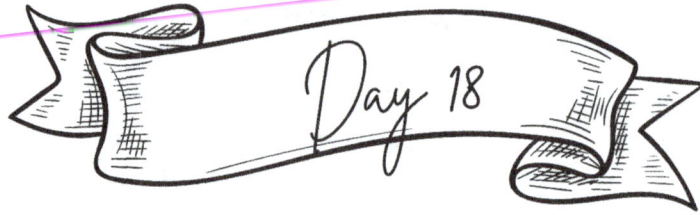

Prideful Attitudes

"Pride goes before destruction, and a haughty spirit before a fall." Proverbs 16:18 (NKJV)

Reflect on the passage...

When you are prideful you are often unwilling to yield or admit your mistakes. This kind of attitude can destroy relationships quickly. However when you are humble you recognize your errors and take responsibility for them. This can improve your relationships with others and draw them closer to God.

Day 18

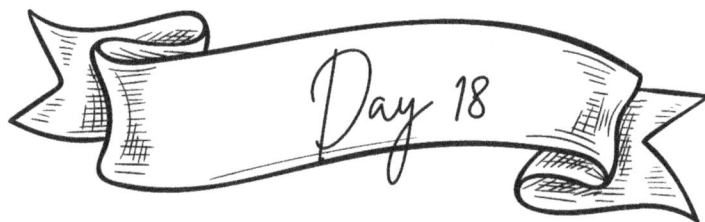

Share your thoughts!

_____

_____

_____

_____

_____

_____

_____

Challenge yourself!

Ask God to help you recognize prideful attitudes. Are there any areas you need to work on? Choose to be humble, open to correction and helpful to others instead. This is God's way!

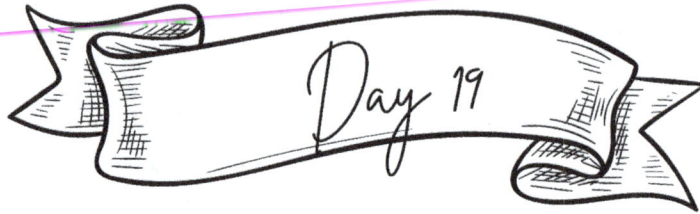

A Friend Loves

"A friend loves at all times, and a brother is born for adversity." Proverbs 17:17 (NKJV)

Reflect on the passage...

Are you a real friend or a fake friend? Sometimes people are there for us as long as everything is going great. As soon as trouble comes, those people go. A true friend is there for you always, no matter what! Be the friend who can be counted on in the good times and the bad times.

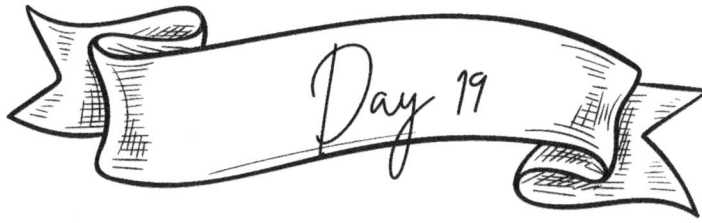

Share your thoughts!

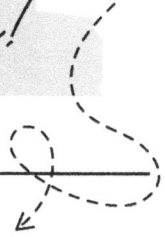

_____

_____

_____

_____

_____

_____

_____

Challenge yourself!

Reflect on your friendships. How can you be a better friend? Reach out to a friend today with a kind word, prayer, or encouragement. There is definitely someone out there who could use a good friend today.

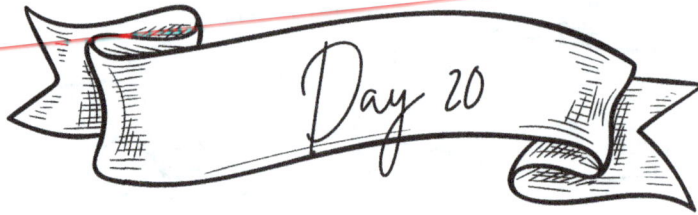

Walking with Integrity

"He who walks with integrity walks securely, but he who perverts his ways will become known."

Proverbs 10:9 (NKJV)

Reflect on the passage...

Integrity means doing what's right, even when no one is watching. Are you a girl who walks with integrity? If you are doing what is right at all times you have peace and you can be confident that you are pleasing God. There is no other way to walk with God. All other paths will lead you astray.

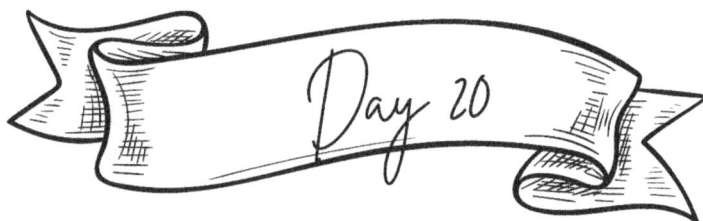

Share your thoughts!

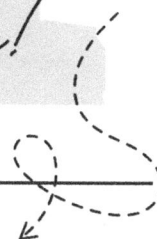

_____

_____

_____

_____

_____

_____

_____

Challenge yourself!

Do your actions measure up to God's standard? Are you trustworthy? Do you have integrity? Can others see that in your life? If you feel even a twinge of guilt about any area, take it to Jesus! He can help you grow into a wise woman of faith.

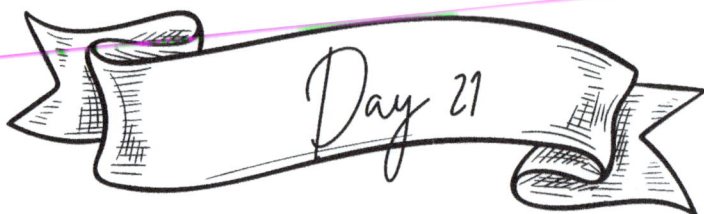

Hard Work Pays Off

"In all labor there is profit, but idle chatter leads only to poverty." Proverbs 14:23 (NKJV)

Reflect on the passage...

Sometimes we don't want to work. It's not that we mind doing work, we just don't want to work too hard or for too long! Another word for that is laziness. The Bible teaches us to work hard and to do all things as unto the Lord. Those who laze around end up getting the reward for their lazy ways. Learn to work hard now so you don't end up on the road to poverty.

Day 21

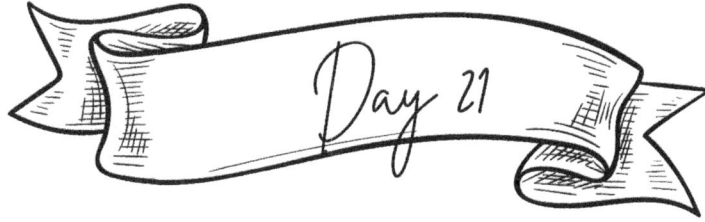

Share your thoughts!

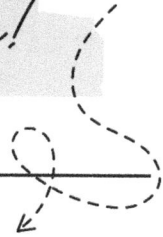

_____

_____

_____

_____

_____

_____

_____

Challenge yourself!

Commit to giving your best effort today. Write down which tasks are a struggle for you. Is it school, homework, chores? Ask God to help you stay focused and plan to work hard until your task is done!

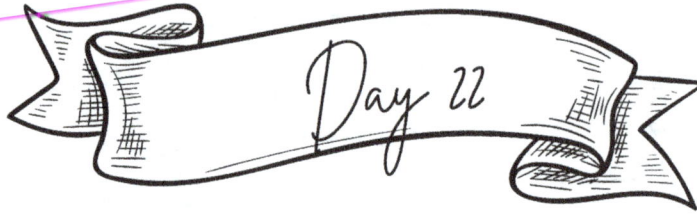

Wisdom Protects You

"Discretion will preserve you; understanding will keep you." Proverbs 2:11 (NKJV)

Reflect on the passage...

Discretion means knowing what to do in a certain circumstance. Remember how we have been talking about wisdom and the Giver of wisdom? How can I know what to do? I need God's knowledge, understanding and wisdom in order to make right choices. He alone knows the end from the beginning.

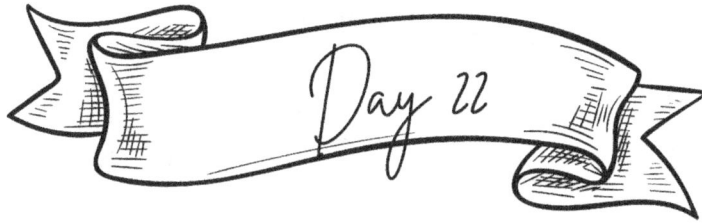

Share your thoughts!

_____

_____

_____

_____

_____

_____

_____

Challenge yourself!

Write down areas where you need discernment, which means the ability to judge well. Maybe it's in choosing friends or who to follow or listen to or receive advice from. Pray about those areas and ask God to help you be wise.

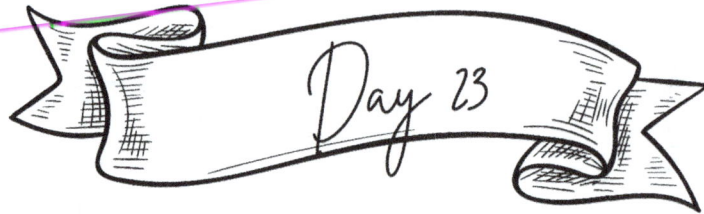

Be Slow to Anger

"A wrathful man stirs up strife, but he who is slow to anger allays contention." Proverbs 15:18 (NKJV)

Reflect on the passage...

Do you struggle with anger? Some do and some don't, but we all get angry from time to time. So what should you do when you find yourself heating up? The verse tells us that when you are quickly angered it only causes conflict, but someone who is slow to anger can keep a conflict from starting.

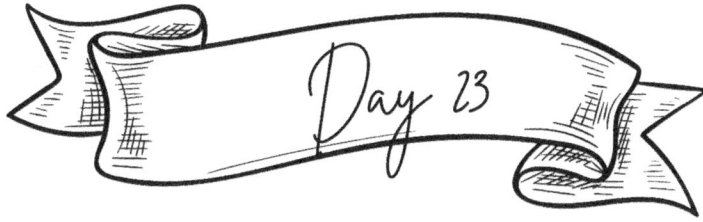

Share your thoughts!

_____

_____

_____

_____

_____

_____

Challenge yourself!

For those moments of anger where you see flames flashing before your eyes don't be quick to respond. Instead, make it your goal to pause and pray. Take time to allow God to work on your attitude (there's that humility sneaking back in), and then you can face the situation with the goal of preventing conflict.

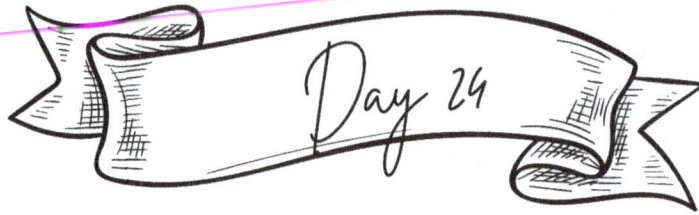

Honor Your Parents

"My son, keep your father's command, and do not forsake the law of your mother."

Proverbs 6:20 (NKJV)

Reflect on the passage...

Why does everyone try to tell you to listen to your parents? Well, the obvious answer would be that since they have lived longer they probably know more about some things than you do. Of course, it could also be that they don't. But God placed your parents in authority over you and the instruction of obeying their instruction is for your good, just like they are commanded to instruct you in the way God has commanded. We don't live in a perfect world, but when both of you are following God's commands your relationship can be sweet!

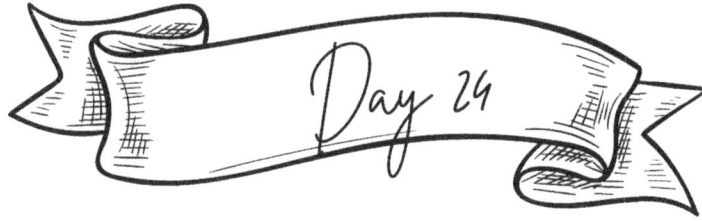

Share your thoughts!

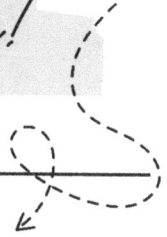

_____

_____

_____

_____

_____

_____

Challenge yourself!

God never says to disrespect your parents just because they aren't doing what is right. Can you think of some advice or instruction that yours have given to you that is helping you today? Thank them for it and strive to honor them in a way that is pleasing to God, and pray for them. They need it too!

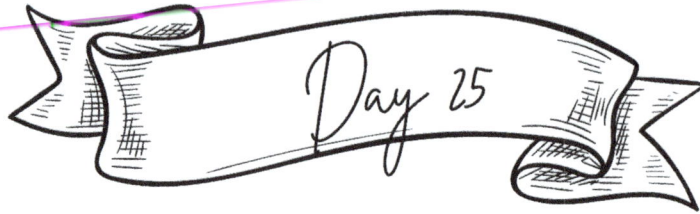

Avoid Gossip

"A talebearer reveals secrets, but he who is of a faithful spirit conceals a matter." Proverbs 11:13 (NKJV)

Reflect on the passage...

No one wants a gossip who tells all of their secrets for a best friend! That would be horrible. Not only should you look for friends who can be trusted to faithfully guard what you share with them, but you should also be that kind of friend. Gossip is to be avoided at all times. If the person is not there to speak for themselves it is often best to leave others' questions and comments unanswered!

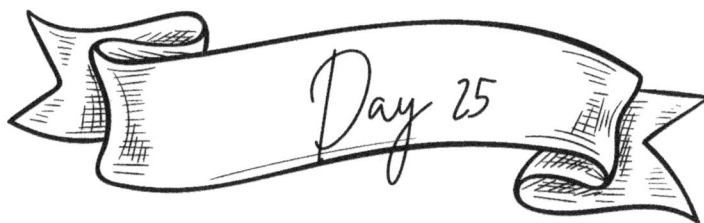

Share your thoughts!

_____

_____

_____

_____

_____

_____

_____

Challenge yourself!

If someone tries to gossip to you gently remind them that the person isn't present so you should wait to talk to them personally or to hear their side of the story. And don't be the one to say, "Have you heard?" Lock up your lips and be a true friend.

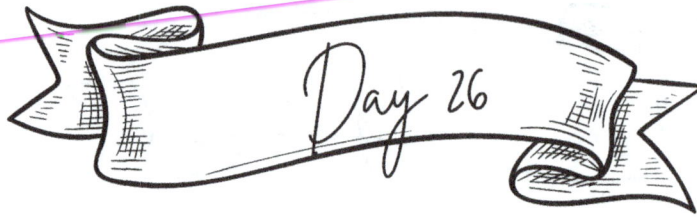

God Directs Your Path

"A man's heart plans his way, but the Lord directs his steps." Proverbs 16:9 (NKJV)

Reflect on the passage...

Today we come back to your hopes and dreams! Remember if you made your plan without asking God what He wants you do with your life, your plans may not turn out the way you imagine. God is the one who is most capable of directing your steps. We must constantly seek Him first and He will guide us every step of the way.

Day 26

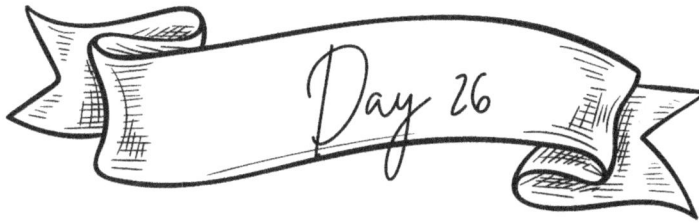

Share your thoughts!

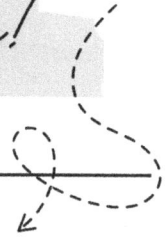

_____

_____

_____

_____

_____

_____

_____

Challenge yourself!

What plans do you have for today, tomorrow, this month, this year? Surrender your plans to God. Take them to Him in prayer and ask Him what you should do. Don't be afraid. He already knows your heart, and everything He does is good.

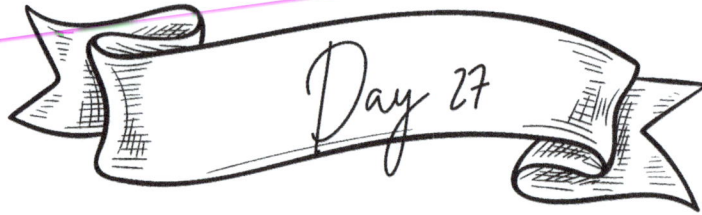

True Friendship

"As iron sharpens iron, so a man sharpens the countenance of his friend." Proverbs 27:17 (NKJV)

Reflect on the passage...

A true friend will encourage you to do what is right. They will challenge you to grow spiritually and to obey God's Word. They truly seek the best for you. If your friend is only concerned about telling you what you want to hear they may not have your best interest at heart. A true friend helps you grow!

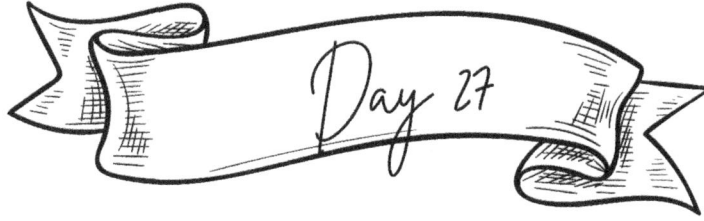

Share your thoughts!

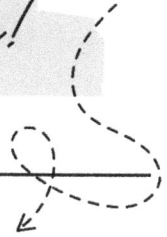

_____

_____

_____

_____

_____

_____

Challenge yourself!

Think about a friend who has "sharpened" you. Reach out and thank them. Write down some ways you can help your friends grow closer to God and try one today.

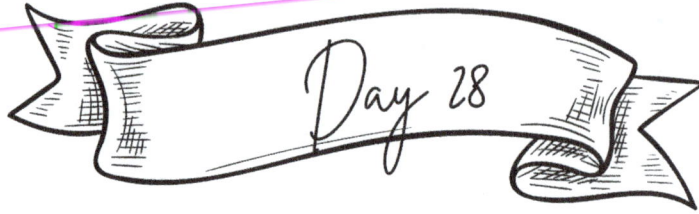

The Best Policy

"Lying lips are an abomination to the Lord, but those who deal truthfully are His delight."

Proverbs 12:22 (NKJV)

Reflect on the passage...

As kids we used to shout, "Liar, liar, pants on fire!" to anyone caught in a falsehood. No one appreciates being lied to, especially God. In fact, he declares lying to be abominable and hateful, but he loves those who tell the truth. Sometimes we lie to avoid trouble or to look good, but none of our excuses are valid with God. A wise woman knows that "honesty is the best policy." There is no other way to live.

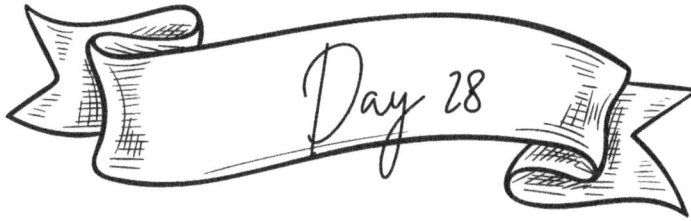

Share your thoughts!

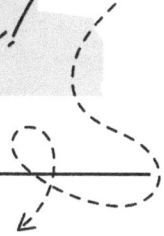

_____

_____

_____

_____

_____

_____

Challenge yourself!

Think back over the last week. Any lies back there? What was your motivation for lying? It doesn't really matter because it was wrong! If you have unconfessed lies, confess them to God now and

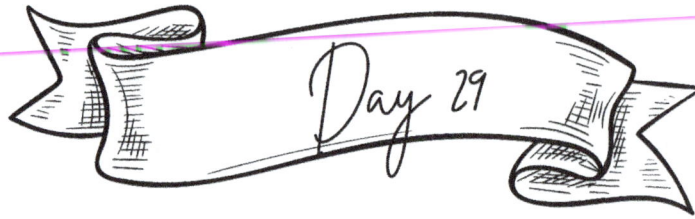

Trust God's Protection

"The name of the Lord is a strong tower; the righteous run to it and are safe." Proverbs 18:10 (NKJV)

Reflect on the passage...

What a blessing to know that our God is a safe place that we can run to in times of need! I like the image of a tower because it automatically represents a place that is secure. The verse mentions that the righteous run to it. Why not the unrighteous? Because they are not seeking God's help or interference in their lives. If you have been going the wrong way, it only takes one step to turn to Jesus. He is the safe place you need!

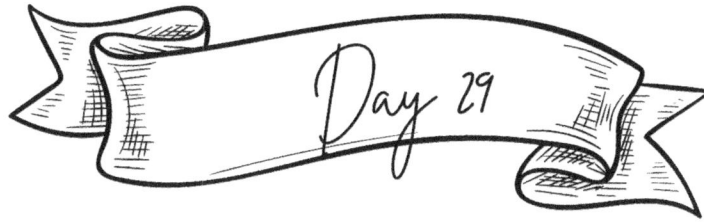

Share your thoughts!

_____

_____

_____

_____

_____

_____

_____

Challenge yourself!

Are you facing fears and struggles? Is your life headed in the wrong direction? Maybe you just need some guidance for today. Write out your needs and ask God to be your strong tower!

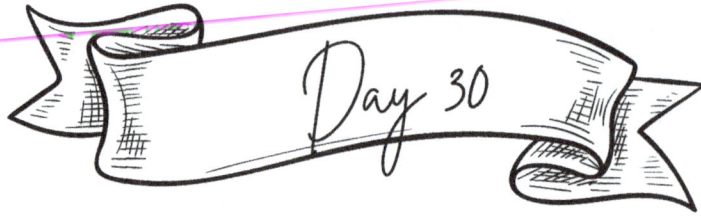

Living for God

"My son, do not forget my law, but let your heart keep my commands; for length of days and long life and peace they will add to you." Proverbs 3:1-2 (NKJV)

Reflect on the passage...

Proverbs is full of wisdom! Our parents can give us wise counsel, but there is none wiser than what we find in God's Word. Keep reading it every day and asking God to give you wisdom and to help you apply it. Your walk with God doesn't stop here. There is more to learn so keep learning and growing. After 30 days you should now have a new habit of studying the Bible so that you can honor God in all you do!

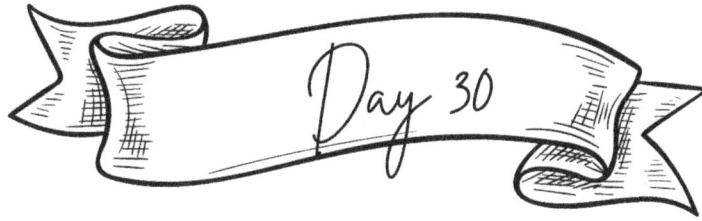

Share your thoughts!

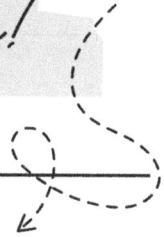

_____

_____

_____

_____

_____

_____

_____

Challenge yourself!

What is the greatest lesson you have learned these past 30 days? Write it down and share it with someone else. Encourage them to also spend daily time with God in study and prayer. Be blessed as you continue to walk with the King!

Notes

_____

_____

_____

_____

_____

_____

_____

_____

_____

_____

_____

_____

_____

Notes

_____

_____

_____

_____

_____

_____

_____

_____

_____

_____

_____

_____

_____

Casandra Pardine is a dedicated pastor's wife, mother, and Bible teacher with a heart for ministry. With 35 years of experience serving in children's and women's ministries, she has been a guiding influence in her local church in New Jersey. Casandra spent two decades as a missionary in Peru, South America, sharing the gospel and mentoring others. A devoted homeschool mom of four, she finds joy in preparing Bible studies that inspire and equip others to grow in their faith.

Made in the USA
Middletown, DE
04 June 2025

76548345R00044